Florida-Backroads-Travel.com

CENTRAL EAST FLORIDA BACKROADS TRAVEL

Second Edition, 2017

Copyright@2015-2017 – D. Michael "Mike" Miller

All Rights Reserved

CONTENTS

INTRODUCTION	1
TOWNS AND CITIES	3
Cocoa	4
Daytona Beach	10
Deland	14
Enterprise	19
Melbourne	22
New Smyrna Beach	26
Ponce Inlet	30
Satellite Beach	35
Vero Beach	38
BEACHES	45
Cherie Down Park	46
STATE PARKS	48
TOURIST ATTRACTIONS	50
Brevard Zoo	51
FESTIVALS	53
HERITAGE AND HISTORY	55

DAY TRIPS AND SCENIC DRIVES　　　　64

- Ormond Beach from Highbridge Road　　65
- Daytona Beach Shores to Ponce Inlet　　66
- New Smyrna Beach to Edgewater　　67
- Oak Hill to Titusville thru Space Center　　68
- Cocoa, Rockledge along Indian River　　69
- Merritt Is Tropical Trl to Georgiana　　70
- Merritt IsTropical Trl to Mathers Bridge　　71
- Indialantic to Sebastian Inlet　　72
- Wabasso to Johns Island on Jungle Trail　　73
- Ft Pierce-Jensen Beach on Indian River Dr　74
- Osteen to Oak Hill on Maytown Road　　75

EPILOGUE　　　　80

Central East

- Daytona Beach
- Port Orange
- New Smyrna Beach
- Titusville
- Rockledge
- Merritt Island
- Cocoa Beach
- Melbourne
- Palm Bay
- Sebastian
- Vero Beach
- Fort Pierce
- Port St. Lucie

VOLUSIA
BREVARD
INDIAN RIVER
OKEECHOBEE
ST. LUCIE

INTRODUCTION

Central East Florida Backroads Travel is your mentor to this region of Florida and its diversity of towns and attractions. Here is a Central East Florida road map to help you plan your trips through this area.

This region starts in the north with **Ormond Beach** and **Daytona Beach** and its International Speedway and world famous beaches. It's center is anchored by **Cape Kennedy**. The Space Age exists contentedly among the old Brevard County towns of Titusville, Cocoa and Melbourne.

Central East Florida is a long narrow region that extends to St. Lucie Inlet in the south. There are only five counties in this region of Florida: **Volusia, Brevard, Indian River, St. Lucie** and **Okeechobee**. All of these counties, except for Okeechobee, have miles of beautiful sand beaches on the Atlantic Ocean.

The culture and history of this region has been influenced by the miles of **Atlantic Ocean** beachfront on the east and the **Halifax River** and **Indian River Lagoon** just a short few miles away from the ocean This region has a maritime and fishing heritage. It has been one of the fastest growing regions of Florida. The **Daytona International Speedway** and **Kennedy Space Center** are modern compliments to the older traditions.

Here is a Central East Florida Road Map to help you plan your trips.

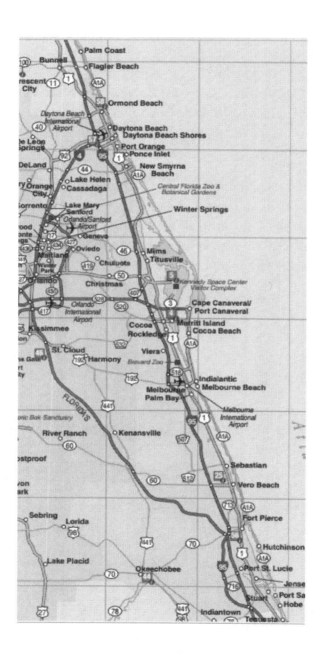

TOWNS AND CITIES

Central East Florida Backroads Travel lists places to stay and eat on the individual town pages. The town pages include a brief history of the town along with my recommended motels, hotels and restaurants. Each town page also includes a description of at least one bed and breakfast or historic hotel.

Some towns and places in Central East Florida included in this edition are:

Cocoa

Daytona Beach

DeLand

Enterprise

Melbourne

New Smyrna Beach

Ponce Inlet

Satellite Beach

Vero Beach

Cocoa

Cocoa is about one hour east of Orlando on SR-528, also known as the **Martin Andersen Beachline Expressway** because it ends up in Cocoa Beach. You go through no Florida towns along the way; it's a straight shot from Orlando to the white sand beaches of Brevard County. We old timers knew it as the **Beeline Expressway** until the tourism promotion people got involved. They wanted the Orlando tourists to know where the beach was.

They didn't really care if people knew that Martin Andersen was the former publisher of the Orlando Sentinel who helped keep the secret of the land purchases being assembled for Walt Disney World.

Cocoa is in the heart of Brevard County and the Space Coast. Take the bridges across the Indian and Banana Rivers and you cross **Merritt Island** to **Cocoa Beach**.

HISTORY OF COCOA FLORIDA

Cocoa was founded by early settlers, mostly fishermen, before the Civil War. The area was first called Indian River City, but the U.S. Postal Department said the name was too long.

Several stories still circulate among Cocoa old timers as to how the town got its name. The version I prefer is the one that said the mail used to come by river boat and was placed in an empty tin box labeled **Baker's Cocoa**. The box was nailed to a piling in the Indian River next to downtown.

In any event, the good citizens got the U.S. Postal Department to accept the name, and the rest is history. It has been called Cocoa since 1884.

One of the earliest hotels in the area was **Cocoa House**. It was located on the Indian River lagoon in downtown Cocoa. Docks and boathouses began to show up as the area continued to develop.

The town was a typical little Florida fishing village until the U.S. government started buying up all the land across the Indian River on **North Merritt Island**. This was in **Sputnik** Cold War era of the 1950's, and they would create a huge missile base. Cocoa's population would soon boom and so would Cocoa Beach.

Kennedy Space Center changed the nature of Cocoa Florida and Brevard County forever. The County grew from 23,653 people in 1950 to 230,006 by 1970. No other place in the United States had ever grown that fast. It may still be a record.

The huge population explosion resulted in a lot of problems. Schools were overcrowded, roads and bridges were congested, and there was a huge housing shortage. The federal government didn't do much to help; it was left to the County and State to solve the problems, along with private developers.

Those problems have been largely solved since the bad old days. It is a fun place to visit and a great place to live.

Today, in 2010, Brevard County has about 530,000 people.

I lived in Brevard County for many years, and have seen much of its transformation. One of the nicest changes has been the rebirth of **Cocoa Village**. This is the name of downtown Cocoa, and it began to redevelop in the early 1970's. What was then a drab little downtown was converted into a beautiful pedestrian oriented village of shops and restaurants.

The born again downtown area attracted several large condominium projects on the river, and the town has become alive and vibrant.

Cocoa is within an easy half hour drive of all major areas of interest in Brevard County. **Cocoa Beach** is to the east,

Rockledge, **Melbourne** and **Palm Bay** to the south, and **Titusville** to the north.

Kennedy Space Center is a short drive to the north.

The drive along the west side of the Indian River from Williams Point through Cocoa Village south to Bonaventure is one of the most beautiful you will ever see. **Sharpes** is a community north of Cocoa where you can still see the weathered old house of **Captain Sharpes**, an early pioneer in this area.

COCOA MOTELS

There are many places to stay in Cocoa, Cocoa Beach and Merritt Island. I'll just focus on a couple that I know something about.

Courtyard by Marriott, 3435 North Atlantic Avenue, Cocoa Beach

Hilton Inn Oceanfront, 1550 North Atlantic Avenue, Cocoa Beach

COCOA RESTAURANTS

The Black Tulip, 207 Brevard Ave, Cocoa. This little fine dining restaurant in Cocoa Village is one of my favorites. Many years ago I saw **America's Most Trusted Man, Walter Cronkite** in there having dinner. He was cruising on his sailboat and staying in a nearby marina. Tel: 321-631-1133

Cafe Margaux, 220 Brevard Avenue, Cocoa. Tel: 321-639-8343. This is right across the street from the Black Tulip, and is also excellent.

COCOA ATTRACTIONS

Kennedy Space Center, SR-405, Kennedy Space Center, FL. Plenty of exhibits and tours. The kids especially love this place. Tel: 866-737-5235

Brevard Zoo, 8225 North Wickham Road, Melbourne, FL. The zoo is home to more than 550 animals representing 165 species from North and South America, Australia and Africa.

Cocoa Beach Pier, 401 Meade Avenue, Cocoa Beach. A Historical Landmark on the Florida Space Coast. Good shops, food, and people watching. It is one half mile north of SR-520 just off SR-A1A.

As mentioned earlier, if you are in Orlando, take the Beach Line to Cocoa. If you are on I-95, take Exit 202 and follow SR-520 east into downtown Cocoa.

Daytona Beach

Daytona Beach is perhaps best known for the **NASCAR Daytona 500** stock car race and as a destination for Spring Break bacchanalia. Daytona Beach is one of the most famous (or infamous) destinations in Florida. It has beautiful beaches and the **Daytona International Speedway**.

Daytona Beach is a mecca for gearheads, hosting numerous racing competitions and events aside from the Daytona 500. The biggest of these events takes place in March. **Bike Week** draws thousands of motorcycle enthusiasts in their best leather apparel to converge on Daytona for 10 days of revelry.

This motorist-friendly attitude permeates all of Daytona Beach; it's one of the few public beaches that allows motorists to traverse its sands. If you're imagining your sunbathing being ground to a halt by a careless motorist, fear not - Daytona offers many pedestrian-only zones.

History of Daytona Beach

The history of Daytona Beach includes some of the first auto races in the United States. It was founded by its namesake **Mathias Day** in 1870. Day was a famous Indian fighter who saw action during the **Apache Wars** against the Apache leaders **Victorio** and **Geronimo**.

Soon after its founding Daytona Beach became a tourist stop on the **Florida East Coast Railroad** of tycoon **Henry Flagler**. In 1926, the cities of Daytona, Daytona Beach and Seabreeze were merged to form present day Daytona Beach.

Since the early 1900s, the smooth hard packed sand beaches of Daytona and **Ormond** have been valued for automobile testing and racing. It was not unusual to see the latest "horseless carriage" or motorcycle being put through the paces on the densely-packed sands.

The Daytona Beach Road Course was the site of the first stock car race in 1936, and led to many more such events. These races and the souped-up hotrods of former moonshiners were instrumental in the creation of that most American of institutions, NASCAR. The NASCAR connection turned Daytona Beach into a mecca for gearheads, hosting numerous racing competitions and events aside from the Daytona 500.

DAYTONA BEACH RESTAURANTS

The Cellar. 220 Magnolia Avenue, Daytona Beach, Florida 32114. Tel: 386-258-0011. Fine Italian dining in an intimate setting. It's in the cellar of a historic home (it really IS a cellar!) and is quite popular for its authentic Italian cuisine and wines, so make reservations.

DAYTONA BEACH HOTELS

Daytona Beach is famous for its oceanfront hotels and motels. These accommodations can be found on Tripadvisor or any of the numerous tourist guides available. In keeping with our site's focus, we prefer to stay at bed and breakfast inns. We recommend the following inn.

The Coquina Inn Bed & Breakfast, 544 S. Palmetto Avenue, Daytona Beach, FL 32114. Tel: 386-254-4969. A cozy four guest room Inn. Nice garden gazebo spa, fresh flowers, cable TV, wireless internet, private bathrooms and five-course breakfast. It is in the Old Daytona National Historic District.

DAYTONA BEACH ATTRACTIONS

Beach Driving. I have been driving on the beaches at Daytona Beach and **New Smyrna Beach** since moving to Florida many years ago. It's great fun to enjoy a slow drive on the hard packed sand beaches and ogle the bathers. These same beaches are where automobile racing was born early in the twentieth century. Driving areas are marked by signs along SR-A1A. Parking is also available on the beach at areas marked by wooden posts. The beach is open to vehicles from sunrise to sunset Nov. 1 through April 30 and from 8 a.m.-7 p.m., May 1 through Oct. 31. There is a $10 per day per vehicle user fee to drive on the beach February 1 through November 30. Residents can also get a beach pass by calling 386-254-4605.

Daytona International Speedway. Famous for the Daytona 500 and other NASCAR races, the Speedway offers hundreds of experiences for the visitor. You can drive a race car, see motorcycle races, run in a half marathon, watch or participate in parasailing, listen to live bands, watch bikini contests and attend autograph sessions featuring famous drivers. 1801 West International Speedway Blvd (US-92), Daytona Beach, Florida.

DeLand

DeLand is just west of I-4 on State Road 44. This small city is at the intersection of US-17 and SR-44 west of Daytona Beach.

HISTORY OF DELAND

DeLand is a city of many firsts. It was visited in 1876 by **Henry Addison DeLand**, a baking soda magnate from New York. He wanted to create a citrus, agricultural and tourism center. He bought large acreage in the area and founded the town, naming it for himself. Henry's dreams went down the drain after the great freeze of 1885. He retreated back north and turned the town's fortunes over to his trusted friend, **John B. Stetson**.

Stetson, creator of the first cowboy hat, made the community his winter home in the late 19th century. His house is now on the **National Register of Historic Places**. Having grown accustomed to the luxuries afforded by his wealth in the modernized north, Stetson soon brought electricity to Florida and DeLand.

He built the state's first electrical plant and ice plant, and the city soon became the first place in Florida to have streets illuminated by the incandescent lightbulb.

Due to this progressiveness, city founder Henry DeLand often referred to his baby as **"The Athens of Florida"**, meaning Athens, Greece, not Athens, Georgia.

DeLand's technological and educational superiority made it the Xanadu of a primitive, undeveloped region.

In 1886, a fire devastated DeLand's business district. The ravenous blaze sparked up in one of the town's saloons and quickly spread to the surrounding wood buildings. The town fathers apparently decided intoxication and fire were a bad combination in those days too, as saloons were thereafter banned from the city.

Don't worry. In modern DeLand, you can get a drink when you need one.

The disaster also led to an ordinance requiring that all new structures be built with masonry instead of wood frame. Thanks to this building code, no less than 68 historic sites can be found within the few hundred acres of historic DeLand. The downtown area is so impressive that the city has won many national and regional "**Best Main Street**" awards.

Majestic oak trees line the streets everywhere, the result of a planting project during the city's formative frontier years. Residents of DeLand received a 50-cent tax break for every oak sapling they planted that made it through one year. There were so many trees planted after the first year that the city couldn't pay its bills and soon had to repeal the law!

The loss of revenue was worth it in the end; the old oaks contrast nicely with the palms in the area and provide better shade from the subtropical heat.

DeLand is a city of murals. You will see them in parks and on the sides of buildings and walls. They are all over town and would make an interesting tour in themselves. Many of them tell stories of the area's history and are beautiful works of art. DeLand is a very artistic city.

Further adding to DeLand's appeal is Stetson University. It seems Stetson is one of a handful of schools competing for the title of "**First College in Florida**". There is no question Stetson had Florida's first law school, established in 1900.

Stetson University was originally called DeLand Academy, but the name was soon changed to Stetson College and later to Stetson University.

The university campus is quite idyllic and has been used as a backdrop for many TV shows and major motion pictures. In fact, many locations in historic DeLand have been used in film and television for their small-town vibe. Take a walk around the district and you're likely to feel as if you've been there before.

DELAND FLORIDA RESTAURANTS

Brian's Bar-B-Que Restaurant, 795 N Spring Garden Avenue, DeLand, Florida. 386-736-8851. Large portions, good service, great ribs. Brian's even has a burger named after John Wayne. You're likely to walk like the Duke too after you saddle up to a half pound of ground sirloin and bacon.

Cress Restaurant, 103 West Indiana Avenue, DeLand, Florida. 386-734-3740. Fusion cuisine. The finest of fine dining, located in downtown DeLand. The freshest ingredients around, because the folks at Cress grow their own produce! Call ahead, this restaurant is small and getting popular.

Shady Oak Restaurant, on the St Johns River at the State Road 44 bridge. Casual dining, beer, wine, fried catfish, hushpuppies and a view of the majestic river as it slowly rolls north toward the ocean.

DELAND FLORIDA ATTRACTIONS

Athens Theater. 1920s era movie house, restored to its former glory. Plays, musicals, concerts and film festivals are frequently held.

Skydive DeLand. Who would guess that DeLand is the skydiving capital of the world? Go here if you want to jump out of a perfectly good airplane. If you're content to watch others kiss the sky, The Perfect Spot restaurant and bar has a good view. Skydive DeLand can be found at DeLand Municipal Airport, which itself has some points of interest as a former World War II base. There's even a campground there.

De Leon Springs State Park. Though it's unlikely the legendary conquistador visited it, this spring's 72º temperature does seem to have restorative powers in the hot Florida summer months. You can also make your own breakfast. Check it out on the Florida State park website. 9 miles NW of DeLand.

DELAND HOTELS

Eastwood Terrace Inn, 442 East New York Avenue, DeLand, Florida 32724. Tel: 386-736-9902. A gracious old historic hotel built in 1925, with suites and guest rooms and private baths. Nice front porch with plants and rocking chairs. Close to DeLand's historic downtown district.

Enterprise

Enterprise is an old village on the southern edge of the modern development of **Deltona**. It is important in the region's early history. This small village is on the north shore of **Lake Monroe** across from **Sanford**. Lake Monroe is a very wide spot in the St. Johns River.

In the early days of Florida's settlement, Enterprise was the last stop for steamers on the St. Johns River. The river was too shallow beyond Enterprise. Passengers had to get off and either stay in a hotel or take the railroad on further east to Titusville. One of the early hotels in Enterprise was the Brock House.

A typical steamer trip from Jacksonville would leave Saturday morning for the 200 plus mile trip up the St. Johns to Enterprise (up is south in the case of the St Johns). Guests would stay in Palatka on Saturday night and arrive in Enterprise on Sunday.

They'd spend Sunday night at Brock House and return back downriver on Monday morning.

Passengers were advised to beware of snakes dropping out of trees as the steamer got close to the river banks. Another hazard was alligators getting tangled up in the steamer's paddlewheel.

Those who wanted to continue on to the east coast could take the train to Titusville. The railroad passed through the small towns of Osteen, Maytown and Aurantia on the way to Titusville. You can still make part of that trip today on **Maytown Road.** This road replaced the railroad tracks years ago and goes through miles of wilderness.

Modern Enterprise is still there, but it's surrounded by the communities of **Deltona** and **DeBary**. The oak canopied streets and some old buildings still make for an enjoyable visit.

One of the old buildings is **All Saints Episcopal Church** at 155 Clark Street. It is on the **U.S. National Register of Historic Places**, and is a Florida example of Carpenter Gothic architecture.

After you've spent a little time looking at the sights in Enterprise, you might drive west to Osteen and take the **Maytown Road** day trip described later in this guide.

Melbourne

Melbourne is a city of about 80,000 people in southern Brevard County on Florida's **Space Coast** about one hour east of Orlando. The city gets its name from Melbourne, Australia. The area began to be called Melbourne eight years before the town was officially established.

A name was needed because a post office was being established to serve families in the area. The first postmaster, **Cornthwaite John Hector**, was an Englishman who spent much of his life in Melbourne, Australia, before opening a general store at Crane Creek. A local pioneer, **Mrs. R. W. Goode**, suggested the post office be named Melbourne.

The area began to thrive in the late 1800s because of its advantageous location on the Indian River Lagoon. Farmers in the area had easy access to a good port and economic transport of their produce to profitable markets.

An interesting local character was **Peter Wright**, a black freedman (a slave freed during the Civil War) who became known as the "**Sailing Mailman**". Wright sailed a regular schedule from Titusville to Malabar on the **Indian River Lagoon** to deliver mail to the numerous riverside settlements.

Melbourne prospered along Crane Creek where it empties into the Indian River, and its fortunes were linked to **Eau Gallie**, another town four miles north of Melbourne with a nice port on the Indian River.

One of the interesting buildings still standing in Melbourne from the early days is the old **Florida Power and Light Company Ice Plant**. It was originally a power generating plant that also produced ice. It is on US Highway 1 near downtown Melbourne, and is on the **National Register of Historic Places**.

Eau Gallie was settled by **William Gleason** and his friends. Gleason had earlier done a lot of development in the Miami area, and was prominent in state and national politics.

The railroad came to Eau Gallie and Melbourne in 1893, and the focus of commerce moved from the Indian River to the tracks on the higher land to the west.

In 1969, local voters consolidated Melbourne and Eau Gallie into one city and picked the name Melbourne for the new venture. Some wanted it to be named **Eau Gallie**; others wanted **Melbogallie** and any other variety of compromise names. We are all grateful that the name Melbourne won out.

Melbourne Restaurants

Chart House, 2250 Front St, Melbourne, FL 32901(321) 729-6558. Beautiful view of the Indian River and Melbourne harbor. Great steaks, seafood and drinks.

Pineda Crossing, 2515 Roberts Road, Melbourne, FL 32940. Tel: 321-259-7760. Great dining in the Suntree-Viera Area: steaks, seafood, full bar.

The "new" Melbourne of today has two distinct "old" and renovated downtown areas: historic downtown Melbourne and **Olde Eau Gallie**, each with lots of restaurants and shops. The old Melbourne Hotel shown on the postcard above still stands on US-1 and is used today as an office building.

The edge of historic downtown Melbourne Florida near the Indian River was the location of the "**Trysting Stairs**, a wooden stairway leading up a bluff at the north end of Front Street.

The stairs provided a convenient way to reach residences on the higher ground above and became an informal meeting place which was especially popular among young lovers at the time.

Melbourne Beach is a short drive Indian River Lagoon. It's a charming little community – the oldest on the beaches - with beautiful sand beaches, good lodging and restaurants. It's a great place to visit and admire some of the older buildings in the village including the **Community Chapel**.

New Smyrna Beach

New Smyrna Beach is a beautiful city of about 20,000 people located about halfway between Daytona Beach and Titusville on Florida's east coast. It's about one half hour drive south of Daytona, and a bit more than an hour's drive northeast from Orlando.

New Smyrna is the vacation destination of choice for many Floridians who live in this part of the state. Many condominiums and cottages in this ocean side town are owned by weekenders from Orlando and the surrounding metro area. The beautiful white sand beaches and deep blue ocean are less than an hour away for most Central Floridians.

A Scottish doctor, **Andrew Turnbull**, founded New Smyrna in 1768. He brought with him about 1500 people of Mediterranean descent, many of them from the islands of Minorca and Majorica off the coast of Spain. Turnbull tried to establish a new colony, and the early settlers tried to grow indigo, hemp and sugar cane. They also tried to make rum.

Conditions were really bad in Florida in those days. The settlers were often attacked by Indians and the insects, including gnats and mosquitos, were abundant and miserable. Most of these settlers abandoned New Smyrna en masse and made the long hike north to St. Augustine, where their ancestors still live. St Augustine was a British possession when this happened, but not long after this became Spanish again.

Dr. Turnbull gave up his colonizing idea and moved to Charleston, South Carolina., where the living was easier.

Both New Smyrna Beach Florida and St. Augustine have lived under four flags: Spanish, British, American and Confederate States of America.

Not much remains in New Smyrna to remind us of Dr. Turnbull and his Minorcan pioneers. There is what looks like the **remains of an old fort** downtown across from the city marina that may be from those days. Nobody seems to know for sure what these ruins are all about. The most repeated theory seems to be that the settlers were building some kind of house or commercial building but stopped work when they bailed out to St. Augustine.

The current Town of New Smyrna Beach Florida was incorporated in 1887. Just 5 years later the **Florida East Coast Railway** came to town and the population of 150 began a steady growth which continues to this day.

The early growth depended on fishing, citrus and tourism. Some growth has been contributed to moonshining and rum running during the Prohibition era in the 1920's and 30's.

New Smyrna's access to the Atlantic Ocean is through Ponce Inlet south of Daytona Beach, formerly known as Mosquito Inlet. New Smyrna Beach has some great white sand beaches that can be driven on just like the ones in Daytona.

NEW SMYRNA BEACH RESTAURANTS

Norwood's, 400 E 2nd Ave, New Smyrna Beach, FL 32169. 386-428-4621. This has been my favorite for years, specializing in seafood. Sad news last time I was in there is that they no longer serve mullet.

The Breakers Oceanfront Restaurant, 518 Flagler Ave, New Smyrna Beach, FL 32169. **Phone:**(386) 428-2019. Good casual dining on the beachfront.

Third Wave Café, 204 Flagler Ave, New Smyrna Beach, FL 32169. 386-402-7864. Trendy, delicious food, great ambiance and outside seating.

NEW SMYRNA BEACH HOTELS

Coastal Waters Inn, 3509 S Atlantic Ave, New Smyrna Beach, FL 32169. 800-321-7882. Direct oceanfront, reasonable rates, close to the beachside dining and entertainment options.

Night Swan Intracoastal Bed and Breakfast, 512 S Riverside Dr, New Smyrna Beach, FL 32168. 386- 423-4940. Mainland in Old Smyrna overlooking the Indian River.

Ponce Inlet

Ponce Inlet is south of **Daytona Beach** on the peninsula bounded by the Atlantic Ocean, Ponce de Leon Inlet and the Halifax River. It's most famous feature is the **Ponce de Leon Inlet Light Station**, built in 1887. This structure has been lovingly restored by a lighthouse preservation society, and is one of best lighthouses to visit in the entire United States.

More than 80,000 people visit the lighthouse every year. The lighthouse is flanked by several brick buildings, including one that houses a museum and gift shop. The lighthouse is the tallest in Florida and is the third tallest in the United States after only Cape Hatteras Light in North Carolina and Cape Charles Light in Virginia.

The lighthouse is open to the public year around and you can climb to the top for a magnificent view of the Florida coast from Daytona Beach to New Smyrna Beach.

The modern settlement of the area began in 1842 when Bartola Pacetti built a driftwood house on 50 acres north of the inlet. Mr. Pacetti was a descendant of one of the immigrants that Dr. Turnbull brought to Florida to settle his New Smyrna colony. The government bought some land from the Pacetti family and built the lighthouse in 1887.

3The population of Ponce Inlet is about 3,000, and the homes range from oceanfront condominiums to modern new homes on heavily landscaped lots. Several of the local streets are unpaved, but easy to negotiate. There are many beautiful tree canopies over most of the streets in town. It is easy to tell that the town has some strict land use and landscaping regulations. They have resulted in one of the most beautiful residential communities in Central East Florida.

What little remains of old historic Ponce Inlet has been lovingly preserved not only by the lighthouse preservation society, but by the **Town of Ponce Inlet** and many volunteers over the years. There is a great little museum on Beach Street that tells the history of Ponce Inlet. The museum is owned and operated by the Town of Ponce Inlet. A very well informed young employee of the town made my visit most interesting and informative.

Fishing has always been a way of life for Ponce Inlet, and the town has several working marinas and boatyards. There are boats to rent and day sails available at several locations along the waterfront.

PONCE INLET PLACES OF INTEREST

Marine Science Center. This is next to the lighthouse and offers information and exhibits on bird and sea turtle rehabilitation. There are nature trails and an observation tower.

Ponce Inlet Jetty. These jetties protect Ponce de Leon Inlet, once known in pre-chamber of commerce days as Mosquito Inlet.

Timucuan Oaks Botanical Garden. This new park is a couple of miles north of the lighthouse and has nature trails meandering through Location: 4550 S. Peninsula. Nature trails wind through the 8 acre garden. It also has a little picnic area.

Ponce Inlet Historical Museum. A small place housed in a restored Florida Cracker duplex. Across the shady tree canopied street is a little pioneer cemetery Great source of local history.

PONCE INLET RESTAURANTS

No addresses or telephone numbers are provided for these restaurants because Ponce Inlet is so small you won't have any trouble walking from one to the other.

Down The Hatch Seafood Restaurant

Hidden Treasure Rum Bar and Grill

Inlet Harbor Restaurant

Jerry's Pizzeria Tiki Bar & Grill

PONCE INLET HOTELS/MOTELS

I don't know of any hotels in Ponce Inlet proper, but there are hundreds of them just north in Daytona Beach. There are a few vacation rentals in Ponce Inlet that can be discovered by doing a Google search.

Satellite Beach

Satellite Beach is a relatively new town by Florida standards. It was incorporated in 1957 and is on the barrier island south of **Patrick Air Force Base** and north of another new town, **Indian Harbour Beach,** founded in 1955. It has a population of about 10,000, and enjoys the Atlantic Ocean to the east and the Banana River on the west.

Brevard County had a severe housing shortage in the 1950s and 1960s due to the rapid build-up of employment at **Kennedy Space Center** in support of the **Apollo** program designed to put a man on the moon by the end of the 1960s. Satellite Beach became one of the residential communities built to handle this extreme demand.

Satellite Beach was founded by **Percy L. Hedgecock**. He and his brother-in-law, **Jimmy Caudle** and cousin **Dumont Smith** were originally from North Carolina and came down to develop real estate in the area. They built many of the original houses in the community. Percy was the mayor of the new town from 1957 to 1973.

Most of the buildings in this little city were built after its founding in 1957, but one old building of interest is **Holy Apostles Episcopal Church** at 505 Grant Avenue.

This church was originally built in Fort Pierce, Florida in 1902 and was barged up the Indian River Lagoon some 60 miles from its original location and placed in Satellite Beach in 1959. So even though the town was only two years old at the time, it had an historic church that is an excellent example of Carpenter Gothic architecture. It was the first church in Satellite Beach.

Satellite Beach today is still largely a bedroom community but one with a tremendous sense of community and some of the best beaches in Florida. These beaches are accessible to the public from one of the many dune cross overs and parks along the oceanfront.

SATELLITE BEACH RESTAURANTS

Niki's Rainbow Restaurant, 570 Highway A1a, Satellite Beach, FL, Satellite Beach. 321-773-8696. Greek food, great taste in a little shopping plaza across from the ocean.

SATELLITE BEACH HOTELS

Radisson Suite Hotel Oceanfront, 3101 N Hwy A1A, Melbourne, FL. 321-773-9260. This is an all suite oceanfront hotel just south of Satellite Beach at Eau Gallie Causeway Boulevard in **Canova Beach**.

Vero Beach

Vero Beach is about 8 miles east of **I-95 on State Road 60**. It is about an hour and a half north of West Palm Beach. It is the place where the tropics officially begin on Florida's east coast. That's not just my opinion; it's a horticultural fact. Tropical things grow in Vero Beach that don't grow even a few miles north of it.

Vero Beach is also at the intersection of **US-1 and State Road 60**. This area near this intersection is almost like a separate town. Beachside Vero - another separate neighborhood - is at the intersection of **State Highway A1A and State Road 60**. Although there are several ways to get there, you will enjoy your visit to Vero Beach no matter which route you take.

History of Vero Beach

The modern history of Vero Beach Florida begins with its establishment as a citrus shipping point. The original name of the community was taken from the Latin word "veritas", meaning truth. The city straddles the Indian River Lagoon, home of the famous Indian River citrus. Citrus was packed in Vero Beach Florida and shipped via the Indian River to Jacksonville and from there to northern ports.

The history of Vero Beach changed dramatically when Henry Flagler's Florida East Coast Railroad made it to Vero in 1893 on its push down the east coast and began the modern era of Vero Beach Florida. Shortly after that developers began to drain the marshy land west of town and created thousands of acres of citrus groves.

These early pioneers foresaw the growth of their little village, and laid it out with wide streets that are now lined with beautiful coconut, royal and date palms. They changed the name from Vero to Vero Beach Florida.

In 1931, Ohio industrialist **Arthur McKee**, who loved the study of tropical plants, opened **McKee Jungle Gardens**. This became a very popular tourist attraction until recent years when part of it was sold for a residential development.

No history of Vero Beach would be complete without mentioning **Waldo Sexton**, a local character and beachcomber, who built his **Driftwood Inn** out of driftwood and other material he picked up off the beach. **The Driftwood Inn** still stands today in Vero Beach Florida. It is now a popular tourist destination known as **The Driftwood Resort** with a good bar and restaurant and plenty of charming time share rooms. It's great to sit by the big pool and enjoy good food, drinks and the ocean.

Vero Beach Florida was also famous as the location of **Dodgertown,** where the Brooklyn/Los Angeles Dodgers baseball team held their spring training camp from 1948 until 2008. It was a sad day for Vero Beach and surrounding towns when the Dodgers moved to a new facility in Glendale, Arizona. The stadium was also the home to the minor league **Vero Beach Devil Rays**.

More bad news came to Vero Beach in August 2008 when the Rays franchise was sold to the Ripken Baseball Group and it was learned the team would not return to Vero Beach for the 2009 season.

Piper Aircraft Inc. has been building Piper airplanes in Vero Beach since 1957 in a plant at the municipal airport. Piper is the largest private employer in Indian River County and is prominent in the history of Vero Beach.

MODERN VERO BEACH HAS THREE DISTINCT AREAS

Beachside Vero on the oceanfront barrier island

Old Downtown Vero on the west side of the Indian River Lagoon

West of Downtown all the way out to I-95 and including the big malls.

Although Vero is the official beginning of the tropics, you will notice it most in the beachside area. You will be surrounded by lush tropical vegetation and fine Florida mansions. The central beach area has its own little shopping district in the area where State Road 60 meets the ocean.

Vero Beach has wonderful beaches. The main beach is accessible from the Central Beach Business District. Many nice restaurants are in this district, along with a couple of motels and

quite a few condos. You will find the beach area of Vero Beach to be more laid back and not as touristy or junky as most other Florida beachside towns.

Old Downtown Vero Beach, on the mainland, is more typical of small Florida towns with the old railroad station and a lot of small retail businesses and antique shops. The area west of Vero Beach straddling State Road 60 has a large regional mall and an outlet mall and many new sprawling subdivisions.

Modern Vero Beach is home to some of the most exclusive golf and marina oriented residential developments in Florida including Johns Island, The Moorings and Grand Harbor.

Vero Beach is reportedly home to more retired **Fortune 500 CEO's** than any other location in the world and has the fourth highest concentration of wealthy households in the U.S. Most of these residents live on the exclusive barrier island that is divided from the mainland by the Indian River Lagoon.

Many of them refer to Vero Beach as **"The Village"**. This designation as "Villagers" does not please some of the old time Vero Beach natives. These wealthy transplants have helped to finance and create many cultural opportunities in Vero Beach.

The **Vero Beach Theatre Guild** started in 1958. The **Vero Beach Concert Association** began presenting concerts in 1966. **Riverside Theatre** opened in 1974, and the **Center for the Arts** in 1986.

Vero also has several entries in the **National Register of Historic Places** including the **Vero Railroad Station, Driftwood Inn, McKee Jungle Gardens** and the **Old Palmetto Hotel**.

Piper Aircraft Inc. has been building Piper airplanes in Vero Beach since 1957 in a plant at the municipal airport. Piper is the largest private employer in Indian River County.

Most business activity other than Piper is tourism or citrus based. Vero Beach's busiest tourist season is from December through April.

VERO BEACH RESTAURANTS

Italian Grill, 2180 58th Avenue, Vero Beach FL 32966. 772-567-6640. Out west between downtown and I-95 near the big regional mall. Great pasta and other Italian dishes, fine Italian dining, good wine selection, nice ambience. I love their grilled chicken and sausage. Pizza appetizers are good too.

Ocean Grill, 1050 Sexton Plaza, Vero Beach Florida 32963. 772-231-5409. This restaurant has beautiful views of the ocean and the food is better than average but not quite great. I have eaten there for 40 years and never had a bad meal. It is a must place to visit in beachside Vero.

VERO BEACH ATTRACTIONS

McKee Botanical Garden, 350 US Highway 1, Vero Beach FL 32962. 772-794-0601. This place is famous for its 18 acre subtropical jungle hammock. This dense and diverse botanical garden also includes several restored architectural treasures. The garden is listed on the National Register of Historic Places and is a historic Florida landmark.

Vero Beach Museum of Art, 3001 Riverside Park Drive, Vero Beach FL 32963. 772-231-0707. This museum is the main visual arts venue in the entire Indian River region. Its neoclassical structure is located in beautiful Riverside Park on the Indian River Lagoon. It has numerous exhibitions, collections, gallery tours, studio and classroom art and humanities education for youth and adults, cinema, community events, lectures, seminars, concerts, dramatic performances and cultural celebrations.

VERO BEACH HOTELS

The area round the I-95 interchange at State Road 60 has several decent chain motels, including **Country Inn & Suites, Holiday Inn Express,** and **Howard Johnson Express**. These motels are eight miles away from downtown Vero Beach, however, and I prefer the places below closer to town. The two places I recommend below are both in beachside Vero.

The Driftwood Inn Resort, 3150 Ocean Drive, Vero Beach, Florida 32963. 772-231-0550. This is a time share resort with rooms available to rent. It is built entirely from ocean-washed timbers and planks, housing some of the world's most beautiful art objects, antiques, and artifacts. It's located in the central beach district on the Atlantic Ocean. The Driftwood offers casual dining inside or poolside at Waldo's Open Air Deck, named after Waldo Sexton, the unique pioneer responsible for building and furnishing the place.

The Caribbean Court, 1601 S. Ocean Drive, Vero Beach, Florida 32963. 772-231-7211. This 18 room boutique inn has beach access and a heated pool. It is located in the choice beach area of Vero Beach. Antique furnishings, hand-painted tiles and original artwork give the room a Caribbean feel. Enjoy live music, tapas and spirits at **Havana Nights Piano Bar** and the extraordinary cuisine of **Maison Martinique Restaurant.**

BEACHES

The beaches along the entire coast of Central East Florida are delightful. Surfers like the area north of **Sebastian Inlet**. **Cocoa Beach** has a wonderful fishing pier with a restaurant. **Daytona** and **New Smyrna** have beaches that you can drive on. Ramps lead from the streets down onto the sand, which is usually firm enough to drive on with no trouble.

Another Central East Florida beach is **Playalinda** at the Canaveral National Seashore. You get there usually through Titusville. It's one of two Florida nudist beaches that I know about. It's not legal to do so, but lots of nudists use Playalinda. Be careful if you have granny and the kids with you. You may have a totally unexpected Florida travel experience.

Every county and city along the coast of Central East Florida have parks and beach access points so the public can enjoy the beach.

Here is some information on a beach that we enjoy in the town of **Cape Canaveral**.

Cherie Down Park

Cherie Down Park is a little hidden treasure on the Atlantic Ocean beach in Cape Canaveral, Florida. It is owned and operated by the Brevard County Florida Parks and Recreation Department.

This little park is a wonderful place to park your car and sit on the beach or take a walk on the sugary white sand. The park is slightly less than 7 acres, and is in a neighborhood setting that makes it perfect for Florida family vacations or beach activities like surf fishing or surfing. Cherie Down Park has one of the best beaches in Florida according to Florida-Backroads-Travel.com. It is one of the best beaches in terms of good walking, good swimming and cleanliness.

Many people also visit the park to watch rocket launches from Kennedy Space Center to the north, or watch cruise ships leaving and entering the harbor at nearby Port Canaveral.

The park has plenty of parking space on most weekdays, but the lot can get filled on winter weekends.

The park has restrooms, a drinking fountain, an outside shower to get the sand off your body, benches, 2 charcoal grills, 2 dune crossovers and a 200 foot long boardwalk paralleling the beach.

There are roofed picnic shelters at each end of the boardwalk so you can enjoy the park even when it rains or when you need relief from the Florida sun.

The park is ADA accessible, with handicap parking spaces, a special dune crossover, paved walkway and restroom features. The picnic shelters can be reserved for special events by calling 321-455-1380. Each shelter can seat 24 people.

The park is open to the public from 7:00 a.m. until dark, except for scheduled use.

Cherie Down Park is located at 8492 Ridgewood Avenue, Cape Canaveral, Florida.

STATE PARKS

There are 13 beautiful Florida State Parks in Central East Florida. These include my favorite, Sebastian Inlet State Park. I have spent many days camping there and fishing from the Sebastian Inlet jetty. Any Central East Florida travel experience will be enriched by a visit to one of the great state parks.

Here are addresses and telephone numbers for Central East Florida State Parks. The parks that I've listed in **BOLD PRINT CAPITAL LETTERS** have full service campgrounds. Some of the others may have no camping at all, or primitive, equestrian or group camping.

Atlantic Ridge State Park, c/o Jonathan Dickinson State Park, 16450 SE Federal Highway, Hobe Sound, FL 33455. 561-744-9814

Avalon State Park, Ft. Pierce Inlet State Park, Ft. Pierce, FL 34949. 772-468-3985

BLUE SPRING STATE PARK, 2100 West French Avenue, Orange City, FL 32763. 386-775-3663

Bulow Creek State Park, 2099 North Beach Street, Ormond Beach, FL 32174. 386-676-4050

Bulow Plantation Ruins Historic State Park, P.O. Box 655 Bunnell, FL 32110. 386-517-2084

De Leon Springs State Park, 601 Ponce DeLeon Blvd. (PO Box 1338), DeLeon Springs, FL 32130. 386-985-4212

Fort Pierce Inlet State Park, 905 Shorewinds Drive, Fort Pierce, FL 34949. 772-468-3985

JONATHON DICKINSON STATE PARK, 16450 S.E. Federal Highway, Hobe Sound, FL 33455. 772-546-2771

Savannas Preserve State Park, Office: 9551 Gumbo Limbo Lane, Jensen Beach, FL 34957. 772-398-2779

Seabranch Preserve State Park, 4810 SE Cove Road, Stuart, FL 34997. 772–219–1880

SEBASTIAN INLET STATE PARK, 9700 South A1A, Melbourne Beach, FL 32951. 321-984-4852

St. Lucie Inlet Preserve State Park, 4810 S.E. Cove Road, Stuart, FL 34997. 772-219-1880

St. Sebastian River Preserve State Park, 1000 Buffer Preserve Drive, Fellsmere, FL 32948. 321-953-5005

TOURIST ATTRACTIONS

There are dozens of popular tourist attractions in Central East Florida, including the following:

Brevard Zoo, Melbourne

Daytona International Speedway, Daytona Beach

Kennedy Space Center, Merritt Island

Port Canaveral, Cape Canaveral

Ron Jon Surf Shop, Cocoa Beach

You can find plentiful resources on the internet to learn more about all of these attractions. Our guide will focus on **Brevard Zoo** in Melbourne, perhaps the largest community built zoo in America.

Brevard Zoo

Brevard Zoo in Melbourne Florida is loved by kids and adults alike. It is one of the most popular Florida zoos. More than 550 animals live here representing 165 different species. Animals are included from Florida, Africa, Asia, Australia and Latin America. Unlike other Florida tourist attractions, you are able to hand feed giraffes and birds, and ride a small train around the grounds.

There is also a guided kayak tour through 22 acres of restored wetlands. You will see giraffes, rhinos, cranes, lemurs and other animals on this tour. Kids enjoy the petting zoo and animal contact zones in a participatory exhibit designed by kids with the help of Robert Leathers.

This beautiful facility was built with a huge volunteer effort. Over 16,000 people helped build it.

I was fortunate to be one of those volunteers in the spring of 1992. That's me in the pith helmet with a feathered friend sometime around that time. This most unique of Florida zoos and tourist attractions opened in March 1994.

It is a world-class zoo where kids and adults learn to understand and love animals. Visiting a zoo is one of the most interesting and relaxing things to do in Florida. Any discussion of Florida tourist attractions is not complete without including Florida zoos.

ADMISSION FEES

Call the zoo at 321-254-9453 for current admission fees. Check with the zoo also for reduced group rates.

HOURS

Brevard Zoo is open daily from 9:30 a.m. to 5 p.m. Last admission is 4:15 p.m. The Zoo is closed on Thanksgiving and Christmas Day. In addition, it closes at 3 p.m. on event days including **Safari Under the Stars**, **Great Tastes of Suntree**, and **Boo at the Zoo** (a Halloween event).

DIRECTIONS

8225 North Wickham Road
Melbourne, FL 32940
321-254-9453

FESTIVALS

Central East Florida art festivals, art shows, folk festivals and other outdoor events are held in some of the most interesting towns in the region. Annual shows take place in New Smyrna Beach, Cocoa Beach, Vero Beach, Melbourne and many other towns and cities.

Here is a partial list of Central East Florida annual art festivals, art shows, folk festivals and other outdoor events arranged by month.

JANUARY

Last Weekend
Images - A Festival of the Arts - New Smyrna Beach.

FEBRUARY (No art shows reported)

MARCH

Second Weekend
Under The Oaks - Vero Beach, Riverside Park.

Last Weekend
DeLand Outdoor Art Festival - DeLand, Florida.

APRIL

Fourth Full Weekend
Melbourne Art Festival - Melbourne, Florida

MAY-OCTOBER No art shows reported.

NOVEMBER

First Weekend

Halifax Art Festival - Daytona Beach, Florida

Second Weekend
Florida Highwaymen Festival - Fort Pierce, Florida

Third Weekend
DeLand Fall Festival Of The Arts - DeLand, Florida

Thanksgiving Weekend
Space Coast Art Festival - Cocoa Beach, Florida

DECEMBER No art shows reported.

HERITAGE AND HISTORY

Central East Florida heritage begins with the early native Americans who dwelled in the area 12,000 years ago. This region was settled by southerners and mid westerners who farmed and fished along the Indian River and Halifax River. This heritage is shared by all counties in Central East Florida. Each county has its fair share of sites that are an important part of Florida history.

Central East Florida heritage and history is an intriguing blend of **Old Florida** and the high tech **Space Age**. The area began to attract settlers in the years immediately following the end of the Civil War in 1865. Prior to that, it was pretty much a "no man's land".

Central East Florida History

The beginning of the space age was at Cape Canaveral in the early 1950's. The heritage is still being made with the space program in Brevard County and the racing legends at Daytona Speedway.

Early settlements were in Ormond, Titusville, Cocoa, Eau Gallie, Melbourne, Sebastian and Fort Pierce. In those early days, life revolved around the Indian River Lagoon. Fishing provided a livelihood, and the communities were tied together by riverboat transportation in the years before the railroad. **Henry Flagler** began extending his railroad south from St. Augustine, and one by one most of these little towns were served by the railroad and began to grow.

The area includes a great diversity of towns and attractions. It starts in the north with **Daytona Beach** and its International Speedway and world famous beaches. It's center is anchored by Cape Kennedy. The Space Age exists contentedly among the old Florida towns of Titusville, Cocoa and Melbourne.

Other old villages were swallowed up when the government purchased the land for the huge Space Center on Merritt Island. Only the old maps and history books will show **Wisconsin Beach, Titusville Beach, Artesia, Audubon** and other places that are now only names.

Central East Florida is a long narrow region that extends to St. Lucie Inlet in the south. There are only five counties in this area of Florida. Two of those counties - Brevard and Volusia - are long and skinny. Together they have more than 100 miles of beautiful sand beaches.

Indian River County and St. Lucie County are smaller, but with equally beautiful beaches. Okeechobee County is landlocked, but has other redeeming features, including Lake Okeechobee.

Central East Florida has several nicknames including **Space Coast** and **Treasure Coast**. It is also referred to as the eastern part of the I-4 Corridor. Interstate Highway I-4 runs from

Daytona to Tampa. This stretch of land from the Atlantic to the Gulf is one of the fastest growing regions in the United States.

Much of the growth is because of Orlando and its major tourist attractions. Families who take in Walt Disney World and Universal Studios also like to spend some time at the beach. Daytona Beach with its speedway and drivable beaches is also a magnet for vacationers. NASCAR fans from all over the country flock to town for major racing events like the **Daytona 500**.

Bike Week in Daytona draws thousands of two wheelers and they are pretty well behaved compared to the image many folks have of bikers. Kennedy Space Center on Merritt Island and its exhibits are also a major draw. Nearby Cocoa Beach has wonderful sand beaches and Ron Jon's Surf Shop.

The St. Johns River, one of the few north flowing rivers in the world, forms much of the western boundary of Central East Florida. This magnificent river is an adventure in itself. It is a fresh water river, and is the longest river in Florida. It is known as the "river of lakes", and is ecologically unique. It forms the centerpiece of much of Central East Florida heritage and history.

Its course is actually a series of what were once salt water estuaries behind the ancient Florida barrier island. Excavations along the St. Johns River have turned up shark's teeth and other salt water souvenirs from ancient times. In ancient Florida history, the ocean was mere yards away from the St. Johns. Now the river is twenty or more miles west of the ocean at most locations.

The St Johns starts in the freshwater marshes of **Lake Helen Blazes** near Melbourne. From there it flows north through

Sanford and discharges in the Atlantic Ocean 20 miles east of Jacksonville. Jacksonville sprawls along the banks of the St. Johns, and its nickname is The River City. The river has played a major role in Florida history.

Harriet Beecher Stowe, who wrote Uncle Tom's Cabin, had a winter home in Mandarin on the banks of the St. Johns River. Many historians feel her novel helped start the Civil War. Abraham Lincoln certainly believed so. Not until the river passes Jacksonville, do its waters become brackish.

The St. Johns River only falls about 30 feet in its 310 mile trip to the ocean. This means it is a lazy river, with slow moving water and lots of meandering. There are many fine little towns and parks along the long scenic course of the river.

The **Indian River** in Brevard County is also scenic and great for fishing and boating. It is really a brackish estuary and is officially known as the **Indian River Lagoon**. It is a large part of Central East Florida Heritage.

Central East Florida Heritage Sites

Here is a list of 141 Central East Florida heritage sites listed by county. The County Seat is also listed.

BREVARD: Titusville

Alma Clyde Field Library of Florida History
American Police Museum and Hall of Fame
Barton Avenue Residential District
Brevard Museum of History and Science
Cape Canaveral Air Force Station
Central Instrumentation Building
Cocoa Main Street

Cocoa Village Playhouse
Community Chapel of Melbourne Beach
Crawlerway
Downtown Melbourne Association
Grant General Store
Headquarters Building
Hotel Mims
Indian River Lagoon Scenic Highway
Kennedy Space Center Visitor Complex
LaGrange Church and Cemetery
Launch Complex 39
Launch Complex 39, Pad A
Launch Complex 39, Pad B
Launch Control Center
Liberty Bell Memorial Museum
McLarty Treasure Museum
Melbourne Beach Pier
Missile Crawler Transporter Facilities
Old Haulover Canal
Operations and Checkout Building
Porcher House
Press Site--Clock and Flag Pole
Rockledge Drive Residential District
Sebastian Fishing Museum
Sebastian Inlet State Park
St. Gabriel's Episcopal Church
St. Joseph's Catholic Church
St. Luke's Episcopal Church and Cemetery
Titusville Commercial District
Valencia Subdivision Residential District
Valiant Air Command Warbird Museum
Vehicle Assembly Building, High Bay and Low Bay

INDIAN RIVER: Vero Beach

City Hall - City of Sebastian Offices
Driftwood Resort
Indian River Citrus Museum Heritage Center
Indian River County Courthouse
Indian River Lagoon Scenic Highway
Laura Riding Jackson Home Preservation Foundation
Maher Building
Main Street Vero Beach
Marion Fell Library
McKee Botanical Garden
Pelican Island National Wildlife Refuge
Pueblo Arcade
Royal Park Arcade
Spanish Fleet Survivors & Salvors Camp Site
Vero Beach Railroad Station
Vero Beach Woman's Club

OKEECHOBEE: Okeechobee

Kissimmee Prairie Preserve State Park
Okeechobee Battlefield

ST. LUCIE: Fort Pierce

Arcade Building
Cresthaven
Fort Pierce Inlet State Park
Fort Pierce Magnet School of the Arts
Fort Pierce Site
Ft. Pierce Main Street, Inc.
Heathcote Botanical Gardens
Moores Creek Bridge

Old Fort Pierce City Hall
St. Lucie County Historical Museum
St. Lucie Village Historic District
UDT Seal Museum
Urca de Lima

VOLUSIA: Deland

African American Museum of the Arts
All Saints Episcopal Church
Amos Kling House
Bethune-Cookman College Historic District
Black Heritage Museum
Blue Spring State Park
Bulow Creek State Park
Canaveral National Seashore
City Island
Connor Library History Museum
Coronado Historic District
Cypress Street Elementary School
Daytona Beach Bandshell
Daytona Beach Partnership
Daytona Beach Surfside Historic District
DeBary Hall Historic Site
DeLand Hall
DeLand Memorial Hospital Museums
DeLand Naval Air Station Museum
DeLeon Springs State Park
Dickinson Memorial Library and Park
Downtown DeLand Historic District
Dunlawton Ave Historic District
El Pino Parque Historic District
Fred Dana Marsh Museum

Gamble Place Historic District
Grace Episcopal Church and Guild Hall
Halifax Drive Historic District
Halifax Historical Museum
Holly Hill Municipal Building
Hontoon Island State Park
Howard Thurman House
Jackie Robinson Ball Park
Lake Helen Historic District
Lippincott Mansion
Main Street DeLand Association
Mary McLeod Bethune Home
Moulton Wells House
Museum of Arts and Sciences and Center for Florida History
New Smyrna Beach Historic District
New Smyrna Museum of History
New Smyrna Sugar Mill Ruins
Nocoroco
Orange City Town Hall
Ormond Beach Community Enrichment Center
Ormond Beach Main Street, Inc.
Ormond Beach Woman's Club
Pioneer Settlement for the Creative Arts
Ponce de Leon Inlet Light Station
Port Orange F.E.C. Railway Freight Station
Rogers House
Ross Hammock Site
S. Cornelia Young Memorial Library
S.H. Kress and Co. Building
Seabreeze Historic District
Seabreeze United Church
Seminole Rest

South Beach Street Historic District
South Peninsula Historic District
Southern Cassadaga Spiritualist Historic District
Southwest Daytona Beach Black Heritage District
Spruce Creek Mound Complex
Stetson University Campus Historic District
Sugarmill Botanical Gardens
Thursby House
Tomoka State Park
Turtle Mound
U.S. Post Office
West DeLand Residential District
White Hall - Bethune-Cookman College
Womans Club of New Smyrna

DAY TRIPS and SCENIC DRIVES

The Central East Florida day trips recommended in this guide are designed to show you some of the most interesting spots off the beaten path in this narrow region.

I-4 is the east-west interstate in this region. It crosses the state of Florida from **Daytona Beach** through **Orlando** to **Tampa**.

I-95 is the north-south interstate in this region. It comes in from Georgia and goes all the way down to Miami and goes through four of the five counties in this region.

The Florida Turnpike is a major toll road on the west side of **Indian River** and **St. Lucie Counties**. The Turnpike starts in Wildwood south of **Ocala** and terminates in **Miami**. A branch of the Turnpike splits off north of Miami and heads south and east to **Homestead** on the way to the **Florida Keys**.

The interstate exits are crowded with gas stations, fast food restaurants and motels. The Turnpike also has oases with gas and food. You can travel the state quickly on these highways (except during rush hours), but not see as much scenery or real towns as you will on our Central East Florida day trips.

The town signs you do see are usually several miles from the downtown section. The fun begins when you get off the turnpike and interstate and hookup with the less traveled roads. There are many state and county highways off the interstate that offer better scenery and a look at real towns. In Florida, some backroads are even four-laned.

The following maps show a few Central East Florida day trips that I recommend:

Ormond Beach from Highbridge Road

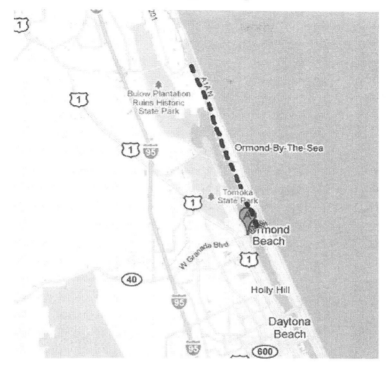

Anderson Drive from Highbridge Road south along the east side of the Halifax River to Ormond Beach. Beautiful river views and tree canopies; fine houses and tranquil neighborhoods. About 9 miles.

Daytona Beach Shores to Ponce Inlet

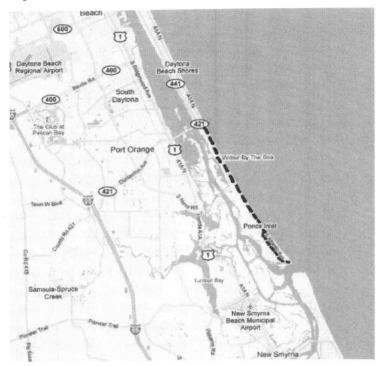

SR-A1A south of **Daytona Beach** from the Port Orange bridge south to Ponce Inlet. End of the road community, great inlet, historic lighthouse, good restaurant. One of the nicest Central East Florida day trips. About 6 miles.

New Smyrna Beach to Edgewater

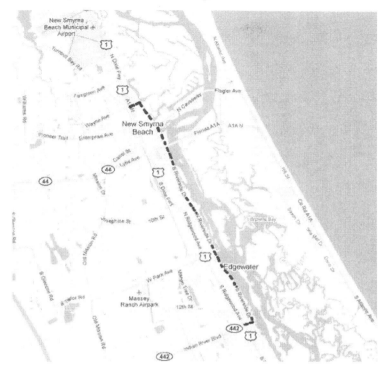

The river road from north **New Smyrna Beach** to **Edgewater**. Close to the river, old houses, beautiful trees. This beautiful scenic route parallels and is on the east side of US-1. You will pass by the city marina downtown and the nice little New Smyrna Yacht Club just north of Edgewater. About 4 miles.

Oak Hill to Titusville through Space Center

Leave US-1 south of Oak Hill and take SR-3 into the top of Kennedy Space Center, then west on SR-406 to Titusville. You will pass a couple of real old pioneer houses in Shiloh, Baker's Haulover Canal south of Shiloh and lots of wilderness and wildlife all enhanced by the mystique of the missile center and the giant looming presence of the Vehicle Assembly Building. About 25 miles.

Cocoa and Rockledge along the Indian River

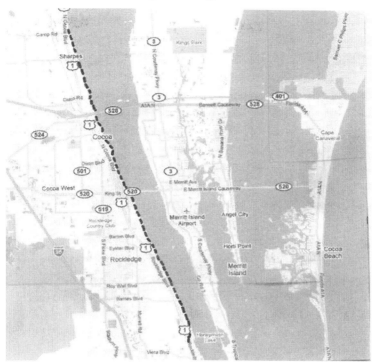

The river road from Williams Point on US-1 north of **Cocoa**, south through Cocoa Village, Rockledge, and Bonaventure. This road parallels US-1, and ties back into it at the south end. One of the most beautiful roads in Florida. Close to the river, some pretty high rocky bluffs in Cocoa, quaint Cocoa Village, fine old houses and big oak and palm trees and lots of Spanish Moss. About 20 miles.

Merritt Island Tropical Trail from SR-528 to Georgiana

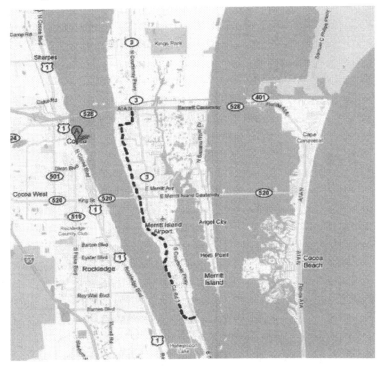

Tropical Trail on Merritt Island from just south of the barge canal to SR-3 at Georgiana. Old Florida that has been bypassed by the newer SR-3. Great old houses and trees. Stop and visit the old Georgiana Methodist church and the nearby cemetery to see the graves of Merritt Island pioneers. About 10 miles.

Merritt Island Tropical Trail to Mathers Bridge

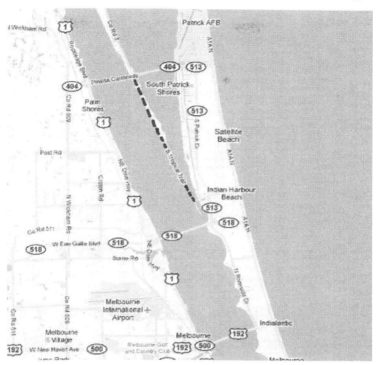

SR-3 from the Pineda Causeway(SR-404) south to the Mathers Bridge at the south end of Merritt Island. This is known as South Tropical Trail. You will enjoy a constant and beautiful Indian River view on your right as you drive along, and stately homes on your left that front on the Banana River. About 4 miles.

Indialantic to Sebastian Inlet

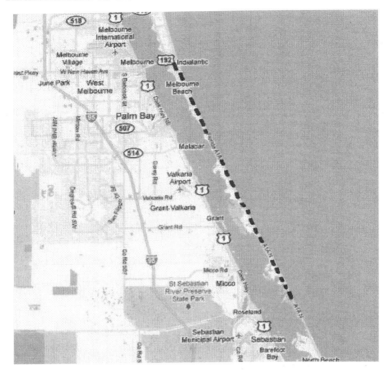

SR-A1A from US-192 at Indialantic south to Sebastian Inlet. Low density development, fine beaches with lots of public access, great fishing and a nice jetty jutting into the ocean at the inlet. About 22 miles.

Wabasso to Johns Island on Jungle Trail

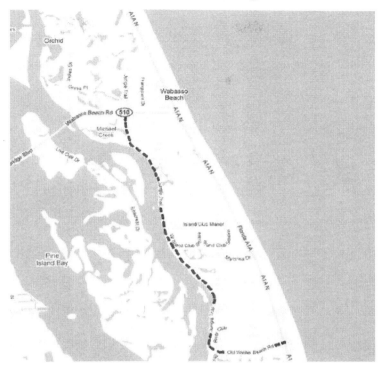

Jungle Trail from SR-510 at Wabasso Beach south along the east side of the Indian River to Johns Island, and back to SR-A1A north of Indian River Shores and Vero Beach. Real old Florida. Was not paved last time I drove it, but easily passable in a normal passenger car. About 4 miles.

Fort Pierce to Jensen Beach on Indian River Drive

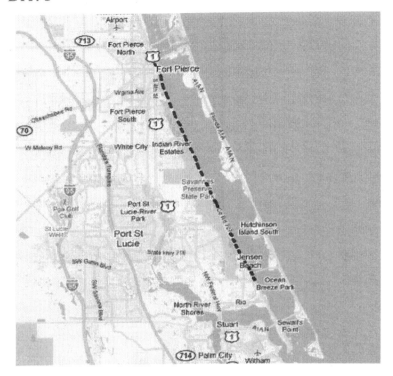

Indian River Drive from Ft. Pierce along the west side of the Indian River to Jensen Beach. Wonderful road hugs the river, beautiful old houses, historic places and magnificent trees. About halfway down you will see the giant St. Lucie nuclear power plant looming up over the barrier island. About 18 miles.

Osteen to Oakhill on Maytown Road

In my early days in Florida, I loved to find deserted roads around the state and just park my car at night and listen to the sounds. The calls of birds, gators, frogs, crickets and bears punctuated the silence. You might hear anything but city and highway sounds.

Those days of 50 years ago are nearly gone. The State's population has quadrupled since I moved here in 1960. It's become crowded and noisy and a traffic nightmare. How depressing!

That's why it's hard to believe that just a few miles from Orlando there is a huge quiet zone that is largely unpopulated. It doesn't really have a name. It's the vast wilderness between Deltona, Sanford and the East coast. It is bounded roughly by

State Road 415 on the west, U.S. Highway 1 on the east, the St. Johns River and State Road 46 on the south and State Road 44 on the north. It's probably 150,000 acres more or less.

The main access through this wilderness is **Maytown Road**. This road starts in the small town of Osteen and heads east across Central Florida to Oak Hill on the Halifax River. It is a lightly traveled paved road. When I first traveled it some 40 years ago it was dirt all the way. It was all too easy to get stuck during muddy conditions. Today it's a breeze to make the drive and it's almost as quiet as it was back then.

There are no real towns in this wilderness. Names of old places that maybe once existed can be found on the maps: **Kalamazoo, Farmton, Cow Creek, Maytown**.

Farmton's name is preserved in the **Farmton Wildlife Management Area**. It straddles Volusia and Brevard Counties and is 59,000 acres. It is privately owned and is used for hunting, grazing cattle and mitigation of environmentally sensitive lands.

Kalamazoo is a private tract of about 11,000 acres that was once planned to be a giant celery farm and self-sufficient village. Pioneers from Kalamazoo, Michigan bought the land and tried to get it started about 100 years ago.

Maytown is a ghost town that used to be a crossroads for two railroads. One of the railroads connected **Enterprise** on **Lake Monroe** to Titusville. The other headed down toward Lake Okeechobee and was known as the **Kissimmee Valley Branch** of the Flagler railroad system.

The railroads are long gone and all that remains in Maytown are a few old abandoned buildings. There is also a pioneer house south of Maytown on a road named Maytown Spur. It's along the old abandoned railroad that ran south toward **Aurantia** and **Titusville**.

Farmton operates under a conservation plan approved by federal, state and local governments. The plan emphasizes sustainable forestry and includes measures to protect wetlands, hammocks and habitat required to preserve wildlife like black bears, bobcats, bald eagles, swallowtail kites and other Florida critters.

Farmton is owned by the **Miami Corporation,** a venture started more than 100 years ago by the **Deering** family of **International Harvester** fame. They still own and manage the lands. The family also built **Viscaya** in Coconut Grove and the **Deering Estate in Cutler Ridge,** hence the Miami connection.

Turnbull Hammock forms much of the eastern border of this large area. Much of it is also protected by conservation areas. The hammock is a huge hardwood swamp and is very difficult to access.

After you've driven through this cool quiet hammock, you will find yourself in Oak Hill. It's a good place for seafood and relaxation. Then turn around and go back the same way.

Make sure you pull off Maytown Road now and then, turn off the car engine and just listen to the quiet. You will be amazed.

DIRECTIONS TO MAYTOWN ROAD IN OSTEEN

From Orlando, find your way to Sanford and take State Road 46 east toward Mims.

Turn left at State Road 415 and go north to Osteen.

Just after the new pedestrian and bike trail overpass, turn right at New Smyrna St.

Follow it back south a block or so until you come to Florida Avenue. Turn left, go east. It becomes Maytown Road. Follow it until you get to Oak Hill.

EPILOGUE

Mike Miller has lived in Florida since 1960. He graduated from the University of Florida with a degree in civil engineering and has lived and worked in most areas of Florida. His projects include Walt Disney World, EPCOT, Universal Studios and hundreds of commercial, municipal and residential developments all over the state.

During that time, Mike developed an understanding and love of Old Florida that is reflected in the pages of his website, **Florida-Backroads-Travel.com**. The website contains several hundred pages about places in Florida and things to do. The information on the website is organized into the eight geographical regions of the state.

Central East Florida Backroads Travel is based on the website. It is one of a series of eight regional guides that can be downloaded in PDF format or purchased as Amazon Kindle or soft cover books. If you find any inaccuracies in this guide, including restaurants or attractions that have closed, please contact Mike at Florida-Backroads-Travel.com and let him know. It is his intention to update the guide periodically and publish updated editions.

If you have enjoyed this book and read it on Amazon Kindle, Mike would appreciate it if you would take a couple of minutes to post a short review at Amazon. Thoughtful reviews help other customers make better buying choices. He reads all of his reviews personally, and each one helps him write better books in the future. Thanks for your support!

BOOKS BY MIKE MILLER

Florida Backroads Travel
Northwest Florida Backroads Travel
North Central Florida Backroads Travel
Northeast Florida Backroads Travel
Central East Florida Backroads Travel
Central Florida Backroads Travel
Central West Florida Backroads Travel
Southwest Florida Backroads Travel
Southeast Florida Backroads Travel
Florida Heritage Travel Volume 1
Florida Heritage Travel Volume 2
Florida Heritage Travel Volume 3
Florida Wineries
Florida Carpenter Gothic Churches
Florida Festivals
Florida Everglades
Florida One Tank Trips Volume 1
Florida Authors: Gone But Not Forgotten

Made in the USA
Columbia, SC
14 August 2018